D1239963

Paper Capers

A First Book of Paper-Folding Fun

Steve and Megumi Biddle

Includes 16 Sheets of Origami Paper

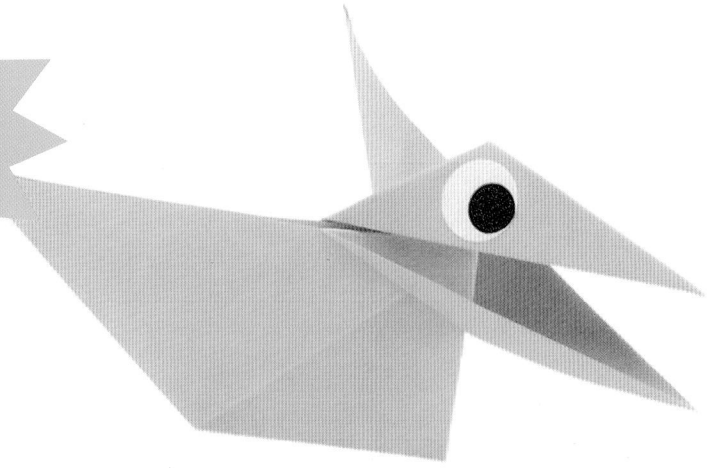

Dover Publications, Inc.
Mineola, New York

WELCOME to the exciting art of paper folding, also called ORIGAMI. Using only paper materials that can be found in almost every home, paper-craft experts, Steve and Megumi Biddle are about to unfold A WORLD OF EXCITING CREATIVITY. *Paper Capers* shows how, with a few helpful hints and tips, you can make STUNNING DECORATIONS, TOYS, GREETING CARDS and unusual gifts from just a few simple sheets of paper!

Origami Tools and Tips

- Make sure your paper is square.
- Fold on a flat surface.
- Make your folds neat and accurate by creasing them into place with your thumbnail.
- Try making the models in the order in which they appear—often the folds and folding procedures are based on previous ones, so you'll find it easier.
- You will need a tube of white glue, a pencil, a ruler, felt-tip pens, sticky tape, needle and thread, and scissors. (Always take great care when handling scissors, keep all tools in a safe place and out of the reach of small children.)

Have fun!

Traditional origami paper is colored on one side and white on the other. In the illustrations the shading represents the colored side. Use *Paper Capers* as the first step toward creating your own origami projects, then why not try experimenting with different types of paper (wrapping paper, for example) or decorate your models with felt-tip pens, glitter, sequins and other crafty bits. And remember, if you are finding a particular fold tricky, don't give up! Just put the model to one side and come back to it another day.

CONTENTS

Bookmark Buddy	3
Xmas Lantern	4
Party Paper Chain	5
Creepy Caterpillar	6
Friendship Bracelet	8
Sensational Stationery	10
Treasure Box	12
Whirly Twirly	14
Pterodactyl	16
Frisbee Flyer	18
Scary Spider	20
Mystery Mask	22
Spinning Top	24
Swan's Nest	26
Fortune Teller	28
Cube	30
Flexi-cube	31

Publisher's Note

The sixteen sheets of origami paper provided at the back of this book will help to get you started making your own paper-craft projects. The origami paper supplied may not be the recommended size or thickness for all the projects in this book. You can purchase additional origami paper, craft paper, or cardstock at your local crafts store, or through online sources.

BOOKMARK BUDDY

Mark the page of your book or diary with this cheeky chappy – he won't let you down!

You will need:
1 square of paper
2 wobbly eyes or
a felt-tip pen
Scissors
Piece of card
Glue

1 Turn the square around to look like a diamond, with the white side on top. Fold and unfold the opposite corners together to mark the diagonal fold-lines, then open it up.

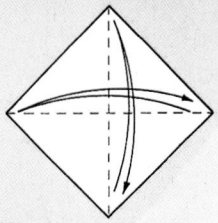

2 Fold three corners in to the middle.

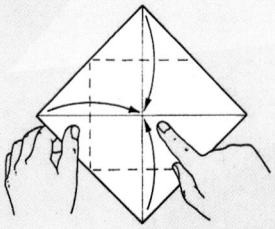

3 Fold the paper along a line from top right to bottom left.

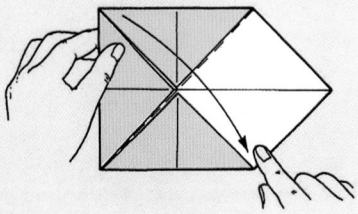

4 Fold the bottom left-hand point up to meet the top point.

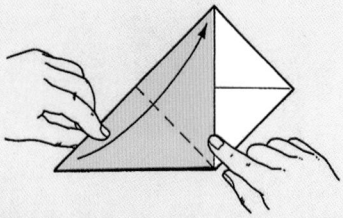

5 Tuck the right-hand point inside the pocket as shown, so making a triangle.

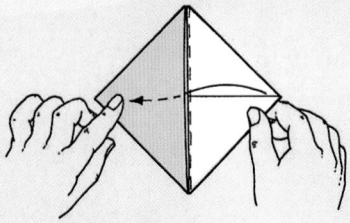

6 Turn the triangle around. Stick on the wobbly eyes or draw on eyes with the felt-tip pen.

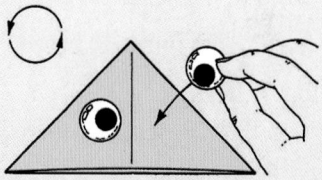

7 To complete the bookmark, cut out a pair of hands and arms from the piece of card and glue them to either side of the model as shown.

Xmas Lantern

This easy-to-make model looks lovely hanging on the branches of a Christmas tree – ideal for a spot of festive fun.

You will need:
1 square of paper
Scissors
Glue
1 strip of paper

1 Fold the square in half from bottom to top, with the white side on top.

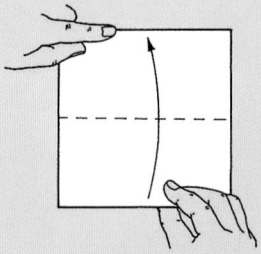

2 Cut strips along the folded edge, towards the opposite edge as shown.

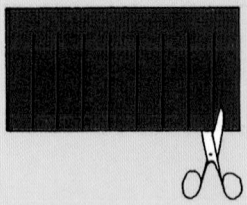

3 Carefully unfold the paper.

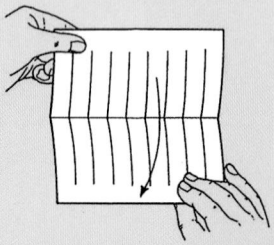

4 Bring the edges of the paper together to form a tube, with the outer strips overlapping.

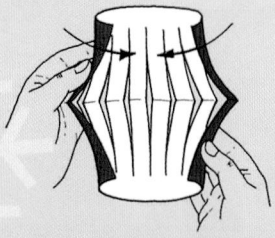

5 Glue the overlapped strips together. Push down on the tube, so that the strips bend outwards a little.

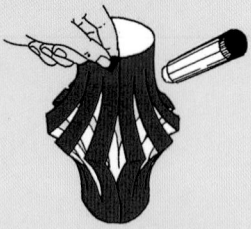

6 To complete the lantern, glue each end of the strip to the top of the lantern as shown, so making a handle.

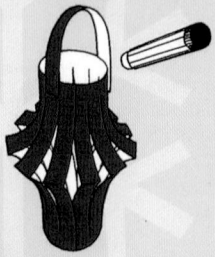

PARTY PAPER CHAIN

Liven up your room with this pretty paper chain – it's perfect for a party!

You will need:
10 or more small squares of paper
Scissors
Glue

1 Begin by repeating steps 1 to 3 of the LANTERN on page 4, with one square.

2 Bring two opposite corners together, so…

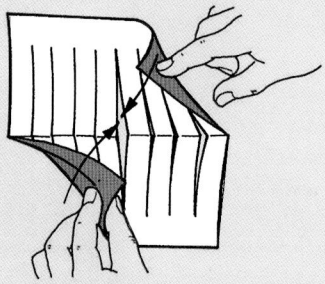

3 that they overlap slightly. Glue them to each other, so completing one piece of the chain.

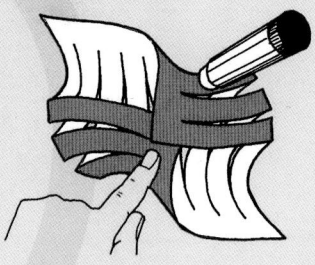

4 Repeat steps 1 to 3 with the remaining squares. To complete the paper chain, glue the pieces together by their corners as shown.

CREEPY CATERPILLAR

Surprise your friends by making this caterpillar jump out of a box. Or leave it trailing down from a shelf...

You will need:
1 square of paper (2 x 2 in.)
Felt-tip pen
2 strips of paper (¾ x 23½ in.)
Glue

1 **Face:** Turn the square around to look like a diamond, with the white side on top. Fold and unfold it in half from side to side.

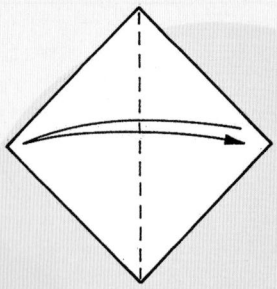

2 From the top point, fold the sloping sides in to meet the middle fold-line, so...

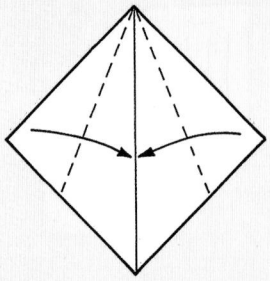

3 making a kite base. Fold a little of the bottom point behind.

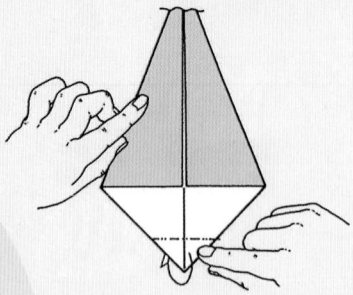

4 Fold the top point down to meet the bottom edge and...

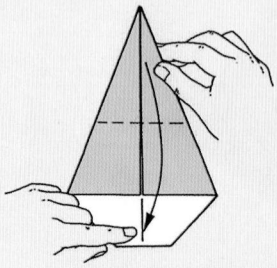

5 fold it back up again, so...

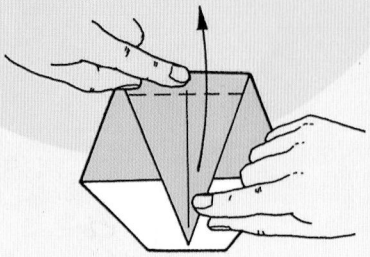

6 making a small pleat.

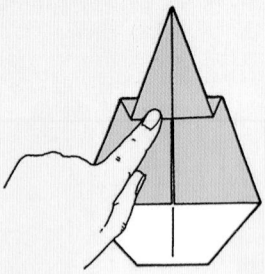

7 Turn the paper over. Fold the top point over. To complete the face, draw on eyes with the felt-tip pen.

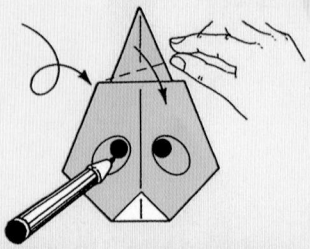

8 **Body**: Using the felt-tip pen, label one strip A and the other B. Apply glue to the end of strip A. Lay strip B at right angles to strip A on to the glued area.

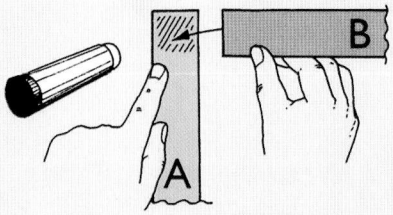

9 Fold strip A up and over strip B.

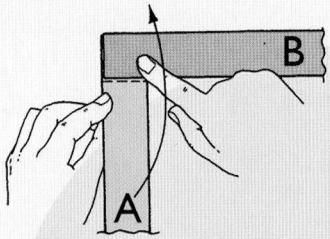

10 Fold strip B across to the left, over strip A.

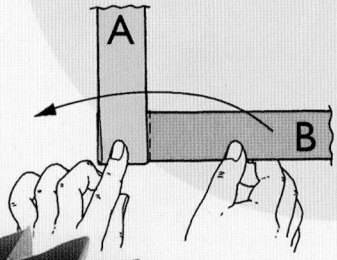

11 Fold strip A down and over strip B.

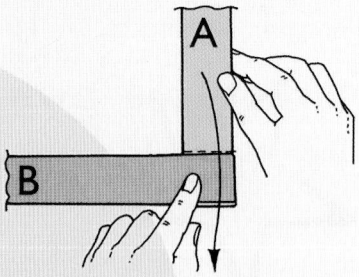

12 Fold strip B across to the right, over strip A. Continue overlapping the strips until all the paper is folded, so completing the body.

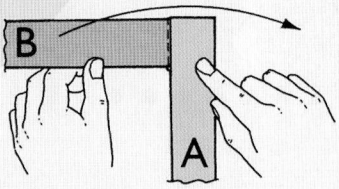

13 Apply glue to one end of the body and attach the face to it. To complete the creepy caterpillar, pull out the body.

FRIENDSHIP BRACELET

Making your own jewelry is easy! And these pretty bracelets are the perfect gift for your special friends.

You will need:
15 strips of paper (¼ x 7¾ in.) in a variety of colors
Needle and thread

1 Turn one strip sideways on. Hold the ends of the strip…

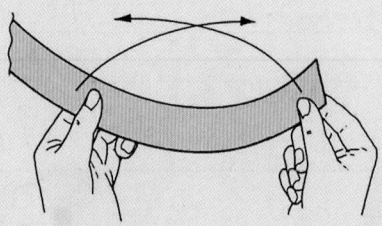

2 and loosely tie…

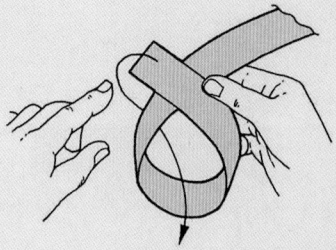

3 a knot at one end.

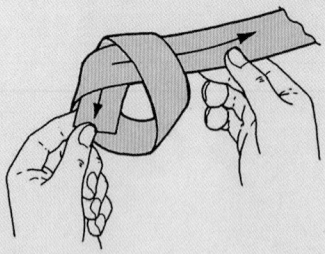

4 Carefully flatten the knot, so making a short and long tail. Tuck the short tail inside the knot.

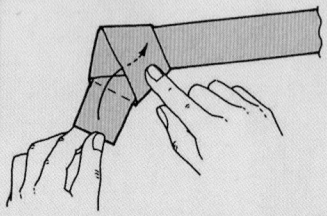

5 Wrap the long tail over the knot.

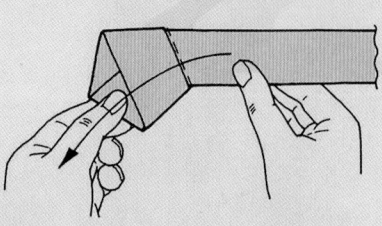

6 Wrap the tail around behind the knot.

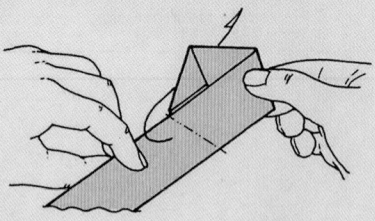

7 Continue wrapping the tail over…

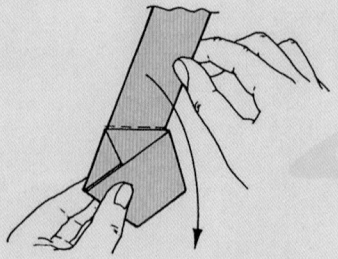

8 and around behind the knot. As you wrap the tail, make soft, not hard folds.

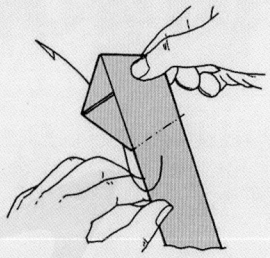

9 Finally, tuck the tail's end in to the knot, so…

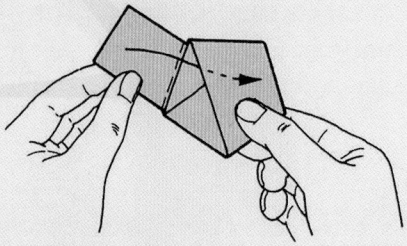

10 making a multi-layered knot. Holding the knot as shown, push in gently the middle of one side, making it indent inwards. Repeat with the remaining four sides, so…

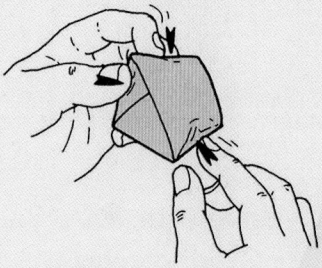

11 making a star-like shape. Repeat steps 1 to 11 with the remaining strips.

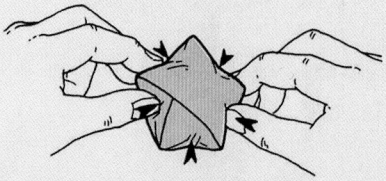

12 To complete the friendship bracelet, thread the stars with a needle (ask a grown-up to help) and tie the ends of the cotton together.

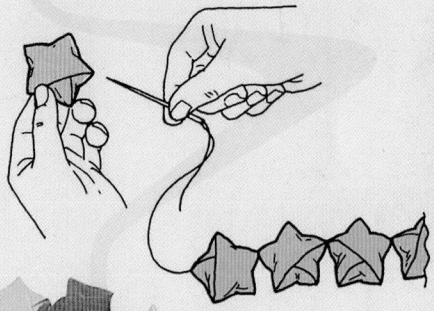

Sensational Stationery

Make your own personal greeting cards and matching envelopes. It's easy with this simple piece of paper-folding.

You will need:
2 8½ x 11 in. rectangles of paper.

1 **Card**: Place one rectangle sideways on. Fold it in half from top to bottom.

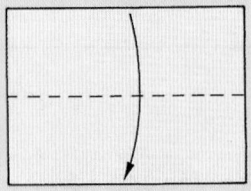

2 Fold in half from side to side.

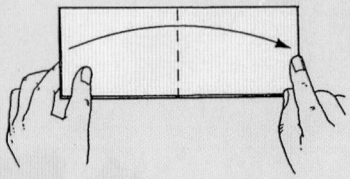

3 To complete the card, press the paper flat. Decorate the front by drawing a picture, or create a design using shapes and patterns cut out from a magazine.

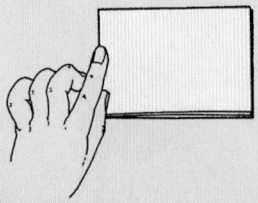

4 **Envelope**: Place the remaining rectangle lengthways on. Fold and unfold it in half from side to side.

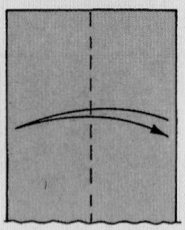

5 Fold the top corners down to meet the middle fold-line, so making a shape that looks like the roof of a house.

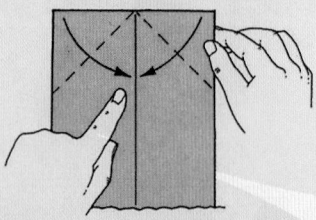

6 Place the card centrally on to the paper, underneath the roof.

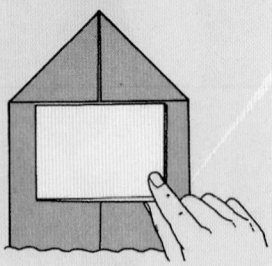

7 Fold the sides in over the card.

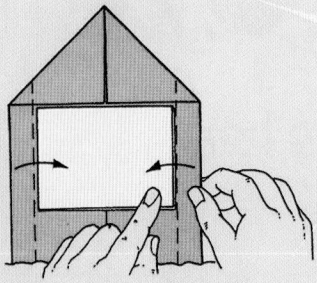

8 Fold the bottom up over the card.

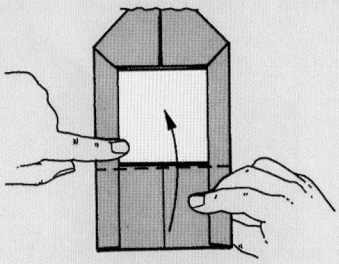

9 Fold the top point down over the card.

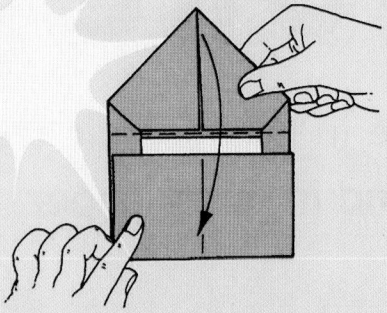

10 To complete the envelope, glue the point down. Now you can decorate it, if you like.

TREASURE BOX

Keep special things safe in this terrific treasure box, or make one for a friend in fancy paper.

You will need:
2 rectangles of paper (one slightly larger for the lid)

1 **Base**: Place one rectangle sideways on, with the white side on top. Fold and unfold the opposite sides and the top and bottom edges, then open.

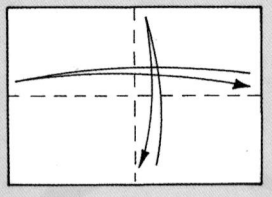

2 Fold and unfold the top and bottom edges in to meet the middle fold-line.

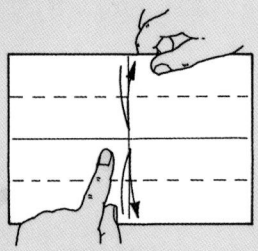

3 Fold the sides in to meet the middle fold-line.

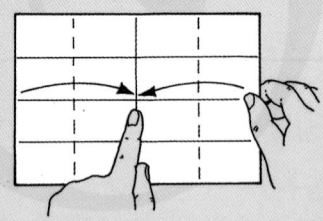

4 Fold the corners in to meet the fold-lines nearest to them.

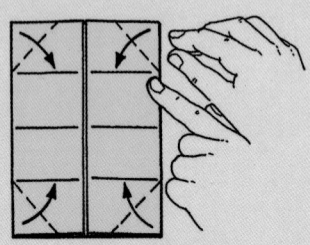

5 Fold the middle flaps back on themselves, pressing them flat…

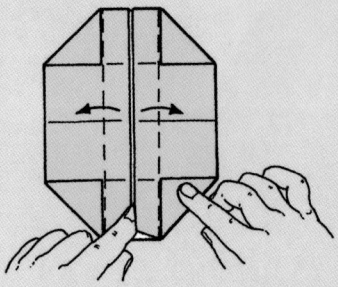

6 over the corners as shown. Put your fingers inside the paper.

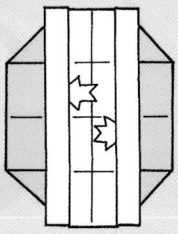

7 Gently pull your hands apart. The paper will start to open out.

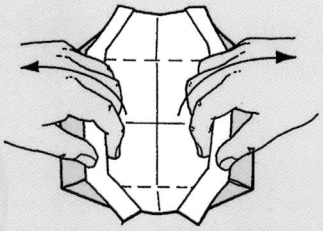

8 Pinch the corners and sides together, so…

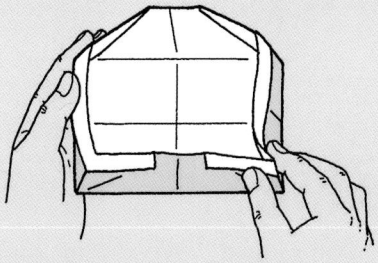

9 making the base firm and strong.

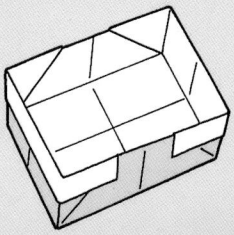

10 **Lid**: Repeat steps 1 to 9 with the remaining rectangle. To complete the treasure box, turn the lid over and slip it over the base.

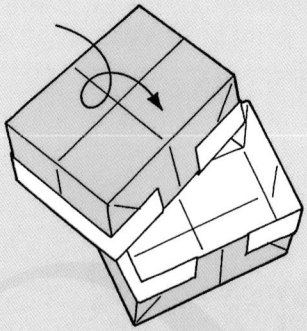

WHIRLY TWIRLY

Make lots of whirly twirlys in different sizes and colors, then have fun flying them with your friends.

You will need:
1 square of paper
Glue

1 Turn the square around to look like a diamond, with the white side on top. Fold and unfold the opposite corners together to mark the diagonal fold-lines, then open it up.

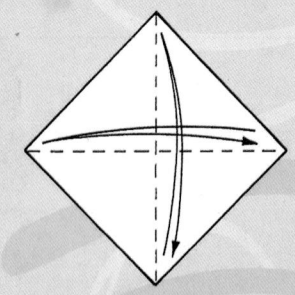

2 Fold the top and bottom corners in to the middle.

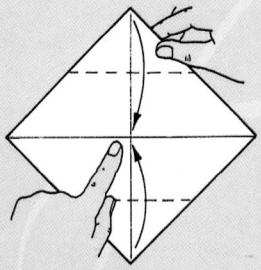

3 Fold the top and bottom edges in to the middle.

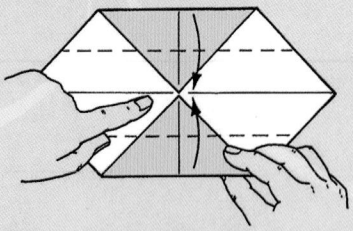

4 Again, fold the top and bottom edges in to the middle.

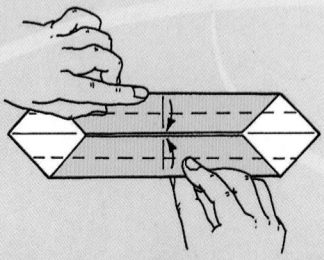

5 Press the paper flat.

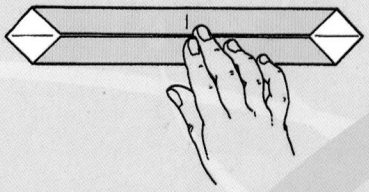

6 Turn the paper over. Apply glue to the left-hand side as shown. Fold in half from right to left and press flat.

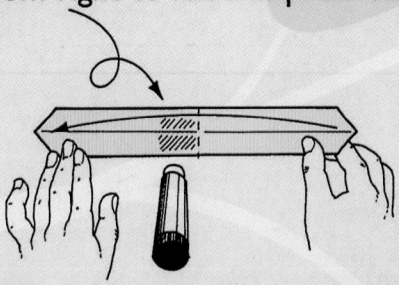

7 Turn the paper around. Fold the topmost flap forwards and…

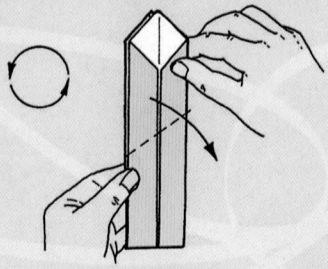

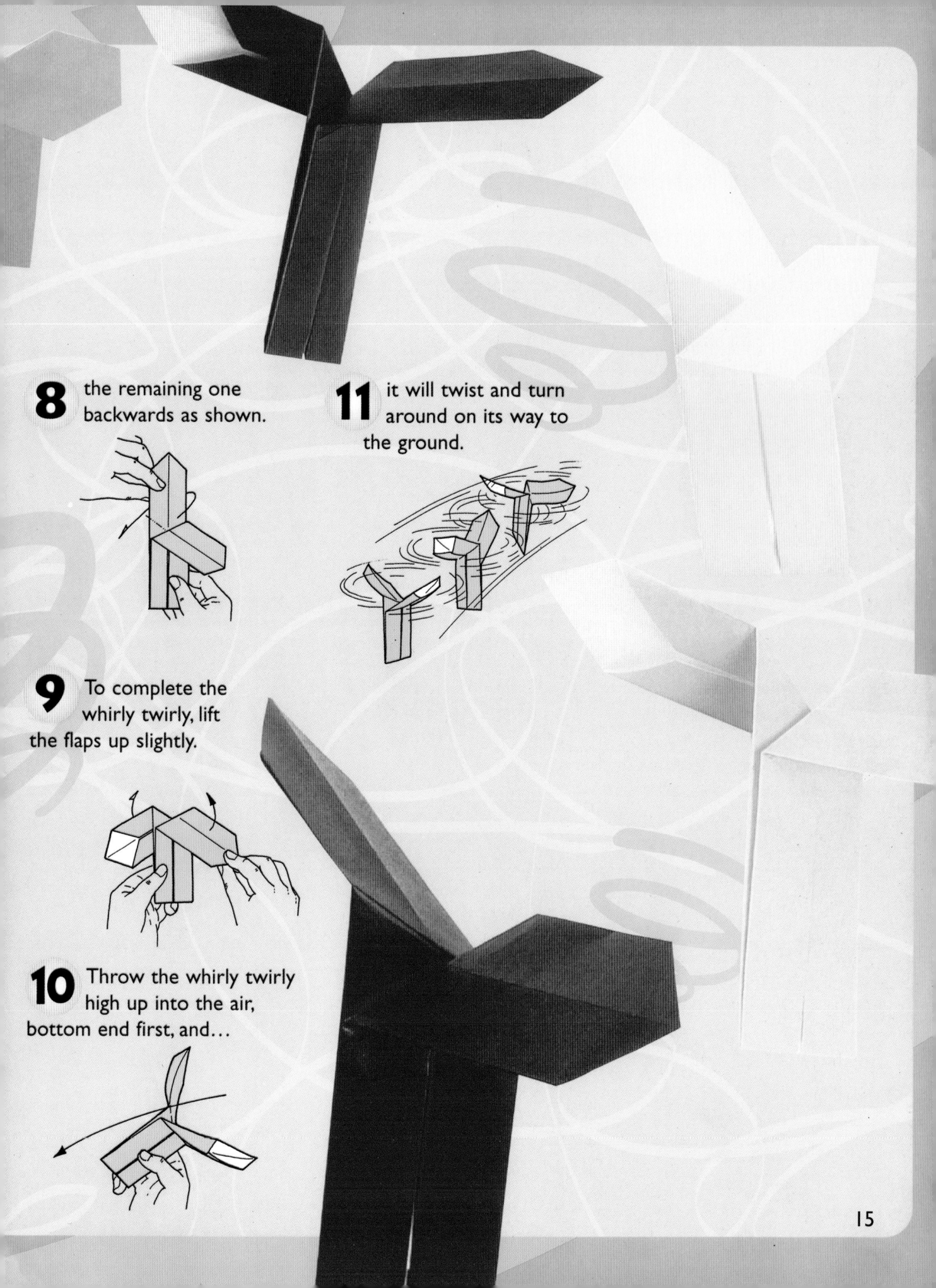

8 the remaining one backwards as shown.

9 To complete the whirly twirly, lift the flaps up slightly.

10 Throw the whirly twirly high up into the air, bottom end first, and…

11 it will twist and turn around on its way to the ground.

PTERODACTYL

You can play a great party game with this pterodactyl – pick up a light object in its beak and pass it to the next person as fast as you can. Whoever drops it must do a dare.

You will need:
1 square of paper
Felt-tip pen

1 Turn the square around to look like a diamond, with the white side on top. Fold it in half from bottom to top, so making a diaper fold.

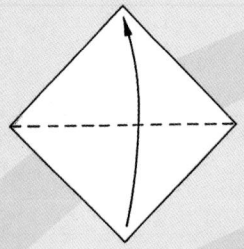

2 Fold and unfold in half from side to side.

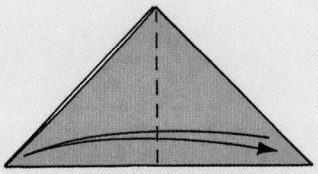

3 From the top point, fold the sloping sides in to meet the middle fold-line.

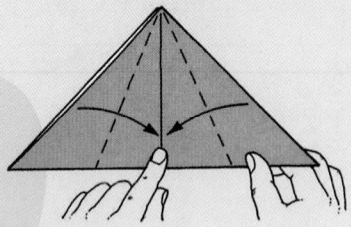

4 Fold the bottom points out to either side.

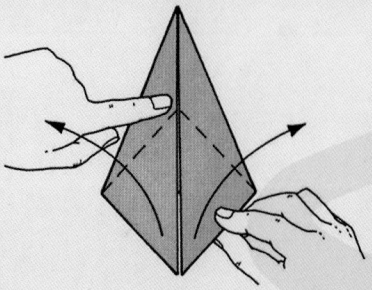

5 From the top point, pull the inside layer out.

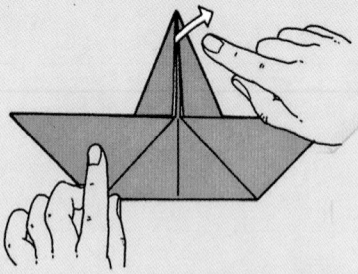

6 Keep on pulling, until you can…

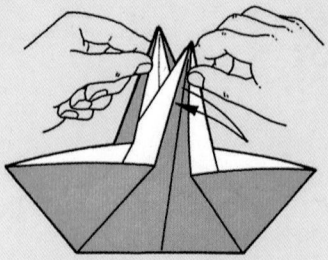

7 arrange the layers as shown. Fold the topmost point down as far as possible.

8 Fold the two points across…

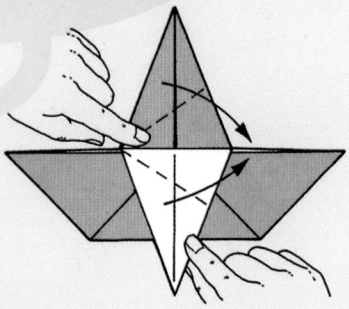

9 to the right.

10 Turn the paper over. Fold in half from side to side.

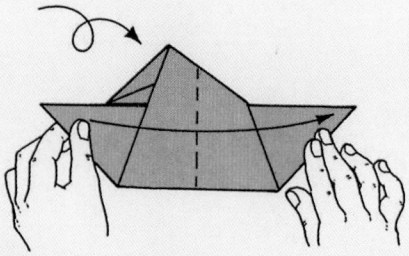

11 Pull the points across to the left and…

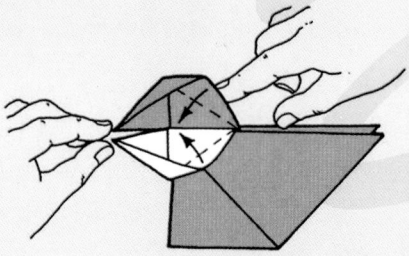

12 press them down neatly, so making the beak. To complete the pterodactyl, draw on eyes with the felt-tip pen.

13 Open and close the pterodactyl's wings to make him talk.

FRISBEE FLYER

This disc will fly through the air, just like a frisbee, so throw it outside where there is lots of space!

You will need:
5 rectangles of thin card (4 x 6 in.) in assorted colors
Sticky tape
Scissors

1 Place one rectangle lengthways on. Fold and unfold in half along a line from top right to bottom left.

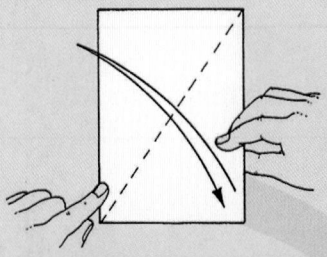

2 Repeat step 1 with the remaining four rectangles. Lay the five rectangles side by side and with tape join them together into a strip as shown.

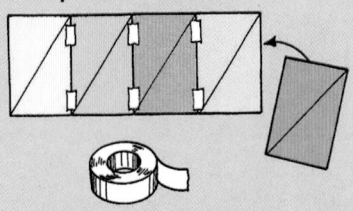

3 Bend the strip around…

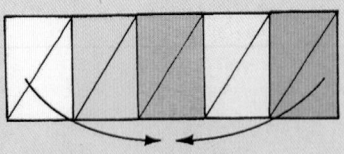

4 into a five-sided tube. Fasten the tube with two pieces of sticky tape.

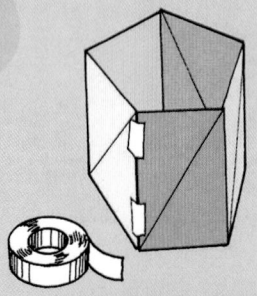

5 Push the tube down from the top and twist it along the fold-lines made in step 1 as shown.

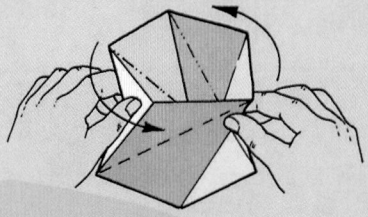

6 Continue twisting and the tube will suddenly collapse flat.

7 Using the scissors, round off each corner.

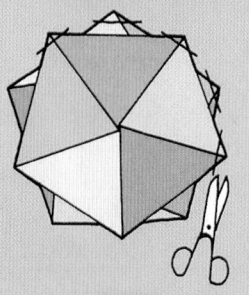

8 To complete the frisbee, and to stop it coming apart, fasten the sides with pieces of sticky tape.

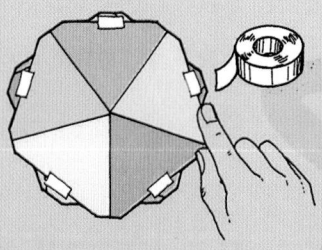

9 Grip one of the frisbee's sides between your thumb and first finger. Release the frisbee by flicking your wrist forward.

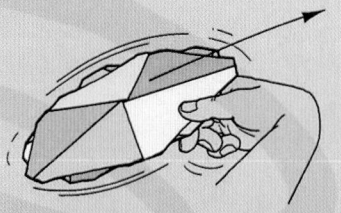

SCARY SPIDER

Make this spider out of fluorescent paper for an extra creepy effect. Hang it in a dark corner, and wait to hear the scream…

You will need:
1 square of paper
Scissors
Glue
2 wobbly eyes or a felt-tip pen

1 **Body**: From the square, cut out a square for the body to the size shown. But don't throw the rest of the paper away just yet.

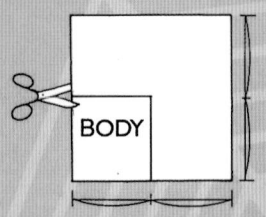

2 Repeat steps 1 and 2 of the CREEPY CATERPILLAR on page 6. Fold a little of the bottom point up.

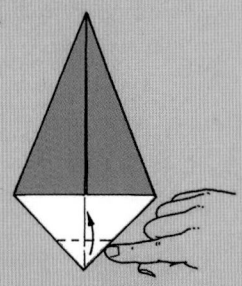

3 To complete the body, fold the top point down as far as shown.

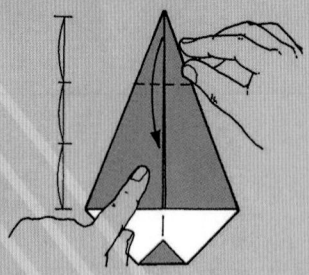

4 **Legs**: From the paper, cut out two rectangles to the sizes shown.

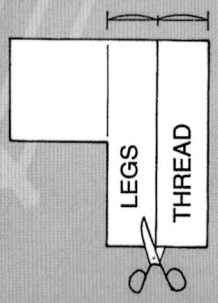

5 Place one rectangle sideways on. Fold in half from left to right.

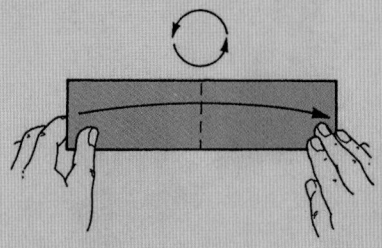

6 From the right-hand side, cut three slits in the paper.

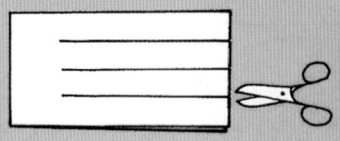

7 Unfold the paper and glue it on to the spider's body as shown.

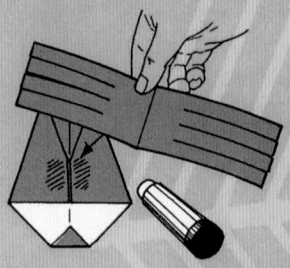

8 To complete the legs, fold them in to shape as shown.

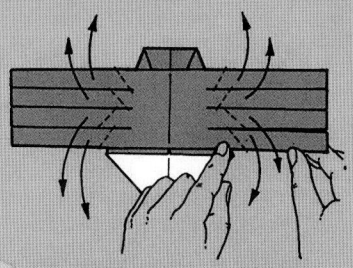

9 Turn the paper over. Stick on the wobbly eyes or draw on eyes with the felt-tip pen.

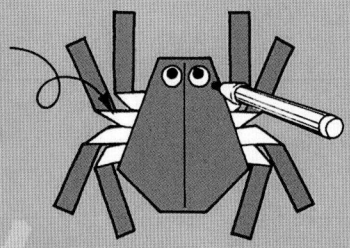

10 **Thread**: Place the remaining rectangle sideways on. Now cut slits in the paper, first from the bottom edge and then…

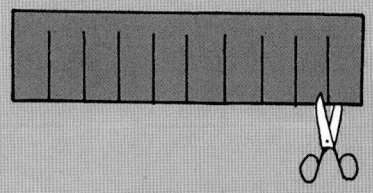

11 from the top edge. Make sure you don't cut right through the paper.

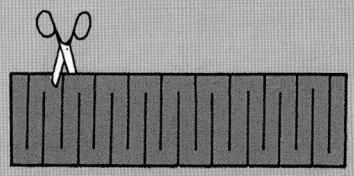

12 To complete the spider, carefully lift one end of the thread up, so as not to tear the paper and…

13 glue it onto the spider's body as shown. The spider will wobble about when its thread is pulled up and down.

Mystery Mask

Become a princess or a pirate! Decorate this basic mask shape with whatever style you like to create a stunning disguise.

You will need:
2 squares of paper
(4¾ x 4¾ in.)
Glue
2 elastic bands

1 Turn one square around to look like a diamond, with the white side on top. Fold and unfold the opposite corners together to mark the diagonal fold-lines, then open it up.

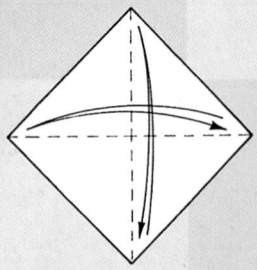

2 Fold the corners in to the middle.

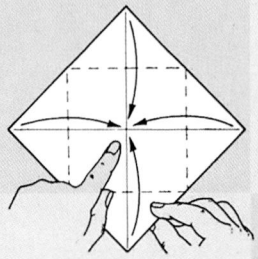

3 Fold and unfold the corners in to the middle.

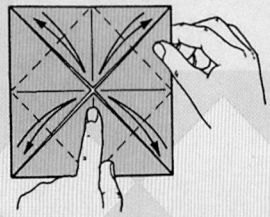

4 Turn the paper over. Fold in half from right to left.

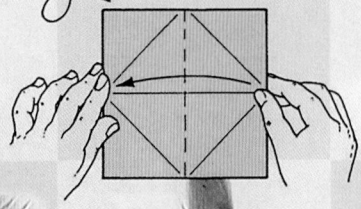

5 Hold the sides together. From the folded side, pull the top section of paper...

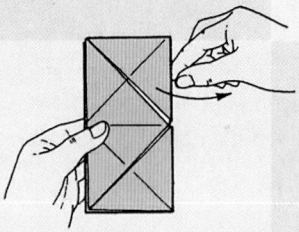

6 outwards, into the position as shown in step 7.

7 Repeat steps 5 and 6 with the bottom section of paper, so...

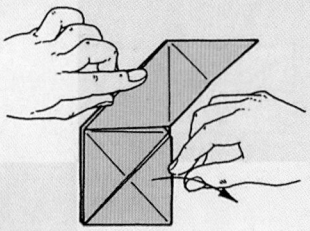

8 making one unit. Repeat steps 1 to 7 with the remaining three squares.

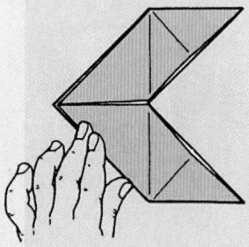

9 The mask is built from a link. To make a link, tuck one unit inside another and glue together.

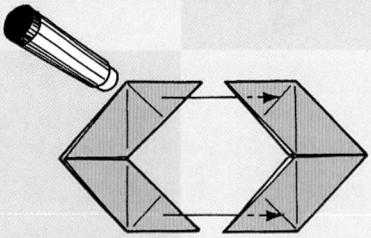

10 It should look like this. Repeat step 9 with the remaining two units.

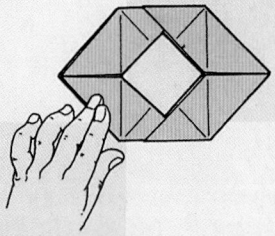

11 Glue the links together as shown.

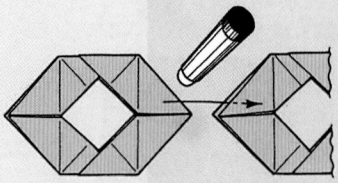

12 To complete the mystery mask, attatch an elastic band to the sides and decorate it with feathers, glitter and sequins.

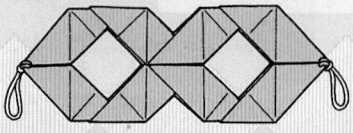

SPINNING TOP

Go spin crazy with these whirling twirling tops. They look extra good if you make them with bright colors!

You will need:
2 squares of paper
1 cocktail stick

1 Fold the bottom edge of one square over to a point one-third of the way to the top, with the colored side on top.

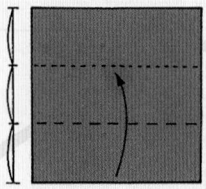

2 Fold the top edge behind to meet the bottom edge.

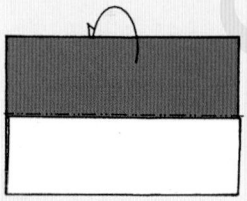

3 Fold the corners of the paper as shown, so...

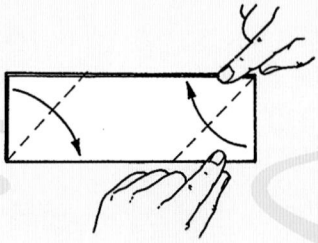

4 completing one unit. Repeat steps 1 to 3 with the remaining square.

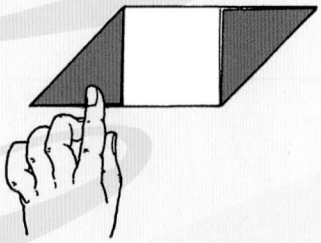

5 Place the units together crossways as shown. Fold the right-hand point over to the left.

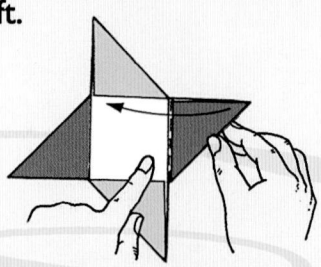

6 Fold the top point down.

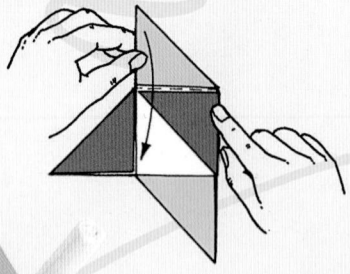

7 Fold the left-hand point over to the right.

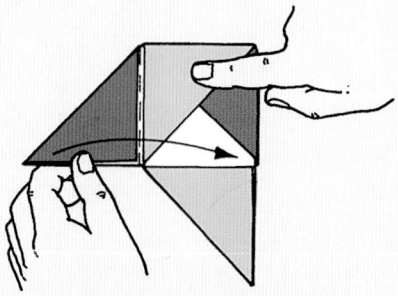

8 Fold the bottom point up, while at the same time tucking it underneath the point nearest to it, so locking the units together.

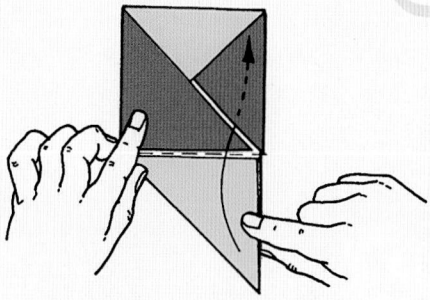

9 Being careful not to stab your fingers, insert the cocktail stick into the middle of the units, so…

10 completing the spinning top. Twist the cocktail stick to set the top spinning away.

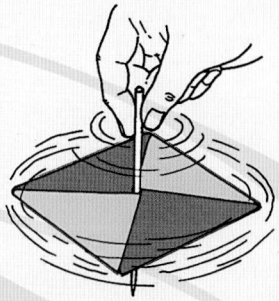

Swan's Nest

This elegant swan can be used to hold anything you like – try adding chocolate eggs for a delicious Easter treat.

You will need:
1 square of paper
Glue

1 Turn the square around to look like a diamond, with the white side on top. Fold and unfold the opposite corners together to mark the diagonal fold-lines, then open it up. Fold the top and bottom corners in to the middle.

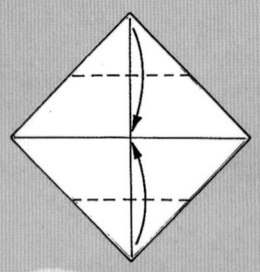

2 Fold in half from bottom to top.

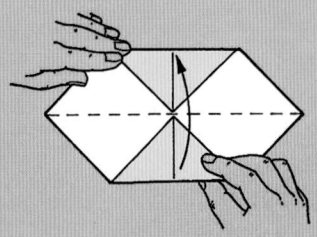

3 Fold the left-hand point up, into the position as shown by the dotted lines. Press it flat and unfold.

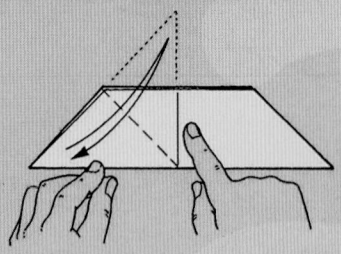

4 Now, using the existing fold-lines as a guide, push…

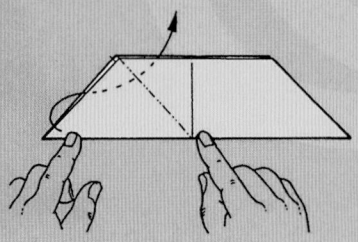

5 the point up inside the model as shown, so…

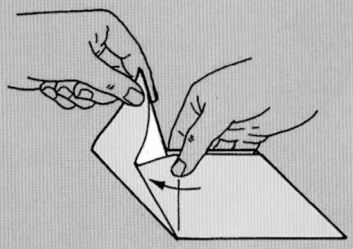

6 making the bird's neck. On either side, narrow down the neck as shown.

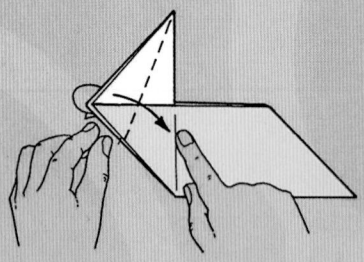

7 Fold the right-hand point up, into the position as shown. Press it flat and unfold.

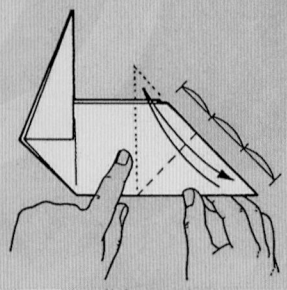

8 Repeat steps 4 and 5, so making the swan's tail.

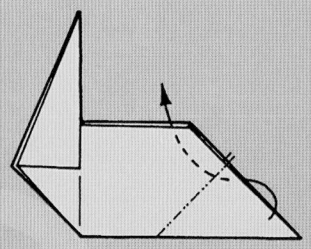

9 Open out the tail.

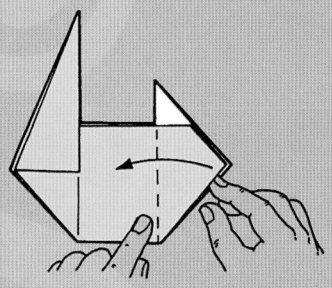

10 Fold the tail's side points in to the middle fold-line. Glue the points down.

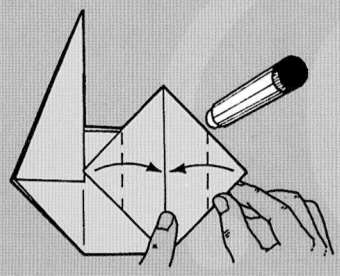

11 Close up the tail.

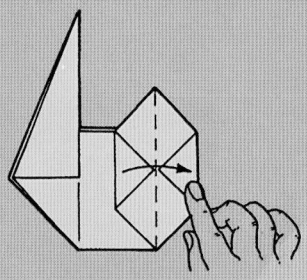

12 Fold and unfold the bottom point as shown.

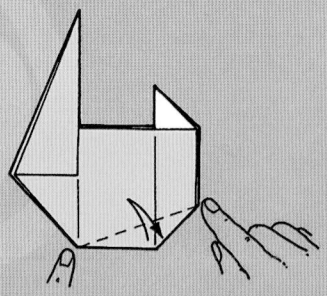

13 Pull the left-hand point down inside itself, so making the bird's head. Open out the model along the fold-lines made in step 12, so…

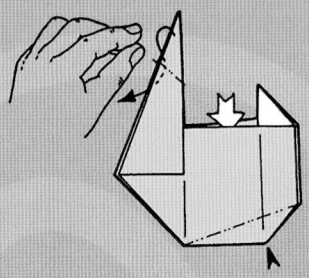

14 completing the swan's nest.

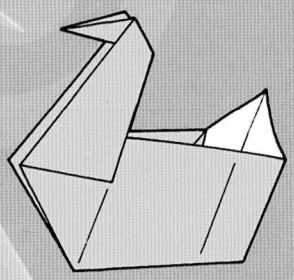

FORTUNE TELLER

Most of us would like to know what is going to happen in the future. With this model you can pretend that you are able to tell fortunes.

You will need:
1 square of paper
Felt-tip pen

1 Begin by repeating steps 1 and 2 of the MYSTERY MASK on page 22.

2 Turn the paper over. Using the felt-tip pen, write a fortune on each square.

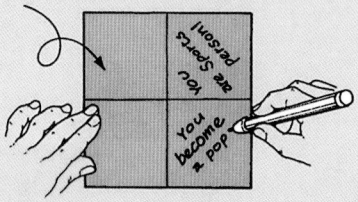

3 Fold the corners in to the middle.

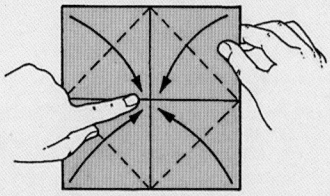

4 Using the felt-tip pen, write the colors blue, green, pink and red on the corners as shown.

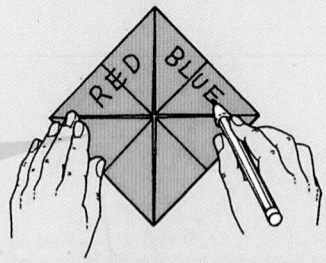

What to write in your fortune teller:

Make your fortunes a mix between real and ideal. *You will become a pop star,* or *You will get an A on your math homework* are some ideas.

5 Turn the paper over. Using the felt-tip pen, write the numbers 1, 2, 3 and 4 on the flaps as shown.

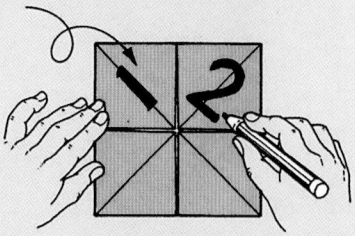

6 Fold the top behind to the bottom along the middle line.

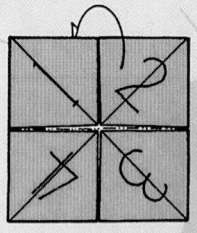

7 Holding the paper as shown, push the sides towards each another, so opening out the paper along its bottom edge, and…

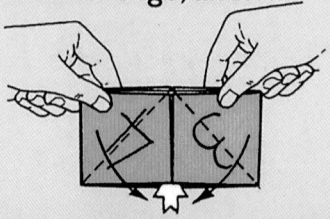

8 collapsing it into a diamond-like shape.

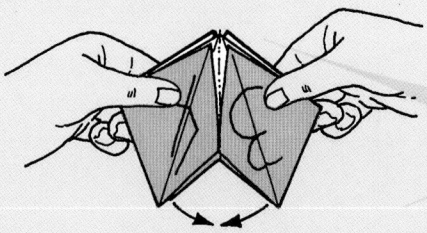

9 Pull out the four flaps and push them in to place as shown, so…

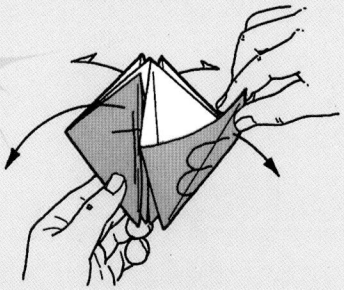

10 completing the fortune teller. Turn the fortune teller over.

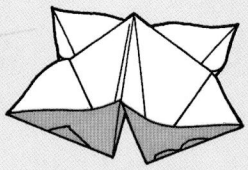

11 **How to tell a fortune**: Place each forefinger and thumb under the flaps as shown. Ask a friend to choose a number.

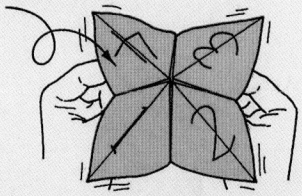

12 Open and close the fortune teller's flaps by pinching the fingers and thumbs together and pushing the flaps outwards up and down…

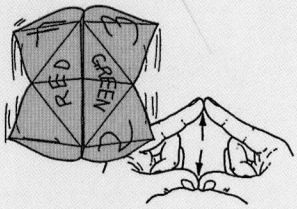

13 and pulling them from side to side for the chosen number of times. Each time you come back to the middle counts as one.

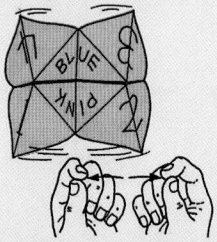

14 Finally, ask them to choose a color, lift up the corner bearing their selection and read out the fortune that is written underneath.

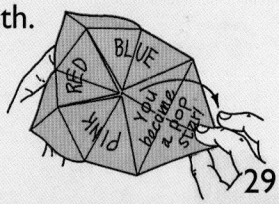

CUBE

There's heaps to do with this chunky cube – start a set of building bricks or use it as a dice.

You will need:
6 squares of paper

1 Begin by repeating steps 1 to 3 of the SPINNING TOP on page 24 with each square. Take two units and join them together by tucking the side point of one into the pocket of the other as shown.

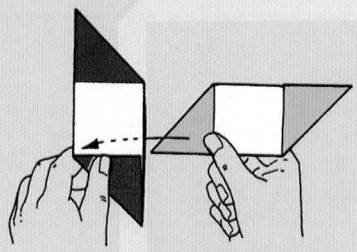

2 Tuck the third unit into place. You are now half way there!

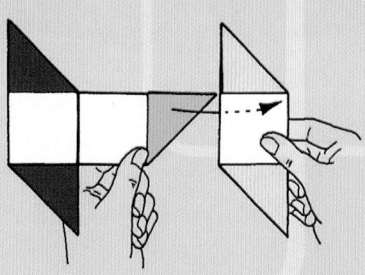

3 Tuck the fourth unit into place. This one is easy.

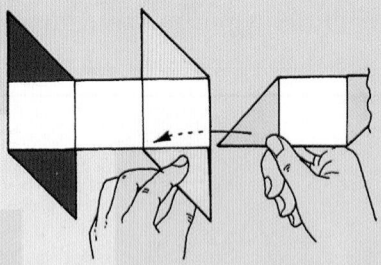

4 To join the units, tuck the right-hand side point into the left-hand pocket. The cube will now begin to form.

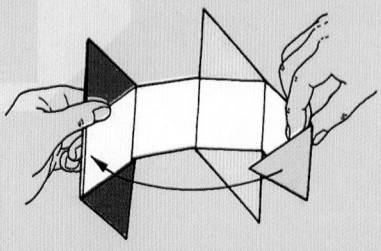

5 From the top, tuck the fifth unit into place by tucking side points into pockets.

6 From the bottom, repeat step 5 with the sixth unit, so…

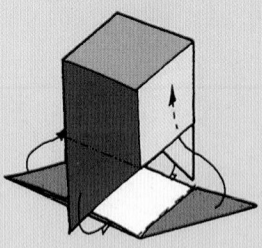

7 completing the cube.

FLEXI-CUBE

The **ultimate** challenge for *Paper Capers* wizards.
Once you can make a flexi-cube, you are ready for anything…

You will need:
48 squares of paper
Sticky tape

1 Begin by making eight cubes – see page 30. Lay four cubes side by side. Join the cubes together along the side with sticky tape as shown.

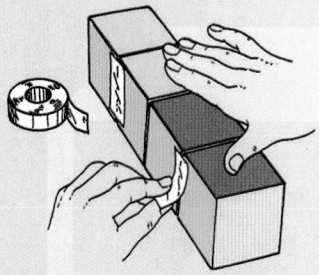

2 Repeat with the remaining four cubes.

3 Lay the cubes side by side in two rows of four, with the sticky tape on the outside.

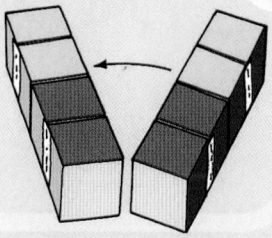

4 Join the cubes together in the center with sticky tape as shown.

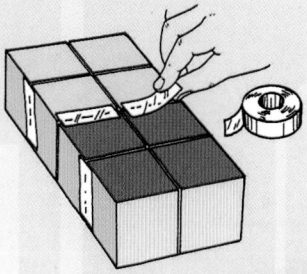

5 Carefully turn the cubes over. To complete the flexi cube, join the cubes together at the ends with sticky tape as shown.

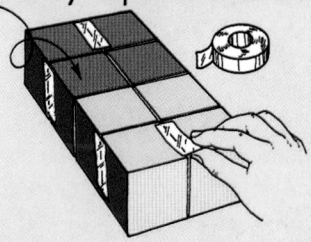

6 Would you like to see the inside of the cubes? Well, flex them inside out and see!

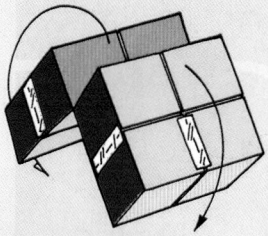

FLEXI-CUBE

CONTINUED...

7 The cubes can be flexed inside out, and . . .

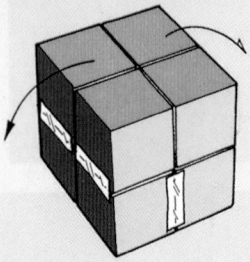

8 over and . . .

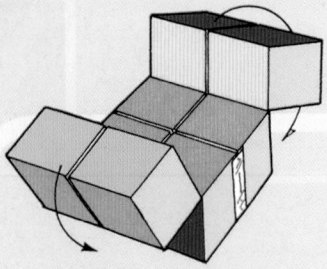

9 over again for as long as you like.

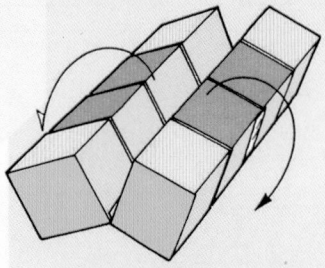

How many combinations can you find?